Virtuous, Victorious & Valued

See Yourself Through the Lens of Christ!

Angela Whitehead

Cover design by Milos Manojlovic
ISBN: 0692396705
ISBN-13: 978-0692396704

Praise and Thanks

I thank my Lord & Savior Jesus Christ for planting the seed of this book in my spirit and keeping it alive until every word was written. I thank my husband Norris and children Niya and Isaiah for their support.

Dedication

This book is dedicated to young ladies all over the world who want to live pure for God. It's never too late to start, or to start over.

Dear Virtuous Queen,

It is my hope that this book will do three things for you. First, I pray it will help you learn what God has to say about the decisions you make in your everyday life. These decisions often seem small but they have a great impact on you. Second, I pray it will help you recognize the tricks the enemy uses to make you feel powerless, desperate and ready to give up on your Christian journey. Remember he only has tricks, but Christ has power! Lastly, I pray this book will equip you with tools that help you recognize who you are, whose you are and what you can do to remain Virtuous, Victorious & Valued!

Blessings,
Angela

CONTENTS

Introduction

Life is what you make it. So why not make it a blast? When I was growing up, I really wanted to be a Christian, but quite honestly, I thought it was too hard. I know that's not what I'm supposed to say, but one thing I promise you in this book is 100% honesty. I won't go off on some religious tangent or spout off a long list of do's and don'ts and Bible verses that leave you feeling like it's impossible to live a Christian life. Instead, I will do three things.

First, I will show you exactly what God has to say about the things you wonder about the most. I'll tell you what God expects of you as a young woman trying to live for Him. No more guessing and trying to figure out what God thinks about sex, temptation, friends, the way you dress, etc. It's all in the Bible! I'll show you where, and how you can implement it in your life.

Second, we'll take a look at the world we live in and examine how everyday things in your life have the potential to make you turn away from God. Things like videos, Instagram posts, and hot music may seem like an ordinary part of day to day life, but they can disguise some nasty tricks the world is trying to play on you.

Third, I'll teach you how to fight. Fight and win! I'll equip you with weapons from God that you can use to fight the things that trip you up on your Christian journey. I call this equipment Royal Resources. These Royal Resources will make it possible for you not to just wish you were a virtuous young woman of God, but actually *live the life* of a virtuous young woman of God. Use the Notes pages in the back to write down the things that really speak to your heart. Get ready. It's going be an amazing ride!

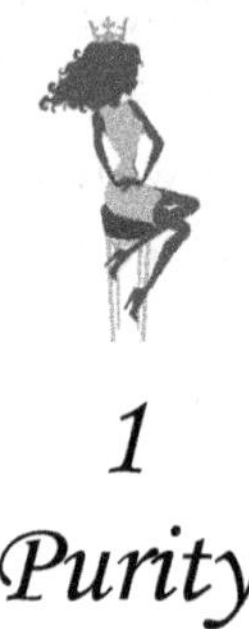

1
Purity

If there's one topic that you have probably been beat over the head with, it's purity. And, for good reason. Too many teens are making the choice to have sex before they are married and with that choice comes a lot of consequences they aren't ready for. That's why churches, youth groups and parents are so adamant about talking to you about sex. But there's a lot more to purity than not having sex.

God has a lot to say about purity. But before we get to that, let's talk about what purity means. Take a minute to think about it and write your definition below.

Purity means ______________________________________

____ .

Relax. There are no right or wrong answers to this question. Let's start by talking about what purity *isn't*. **Purity isn't perfection!** Perfection is something you can never attain. So stop trying! God knows you can't be perfect. He made you for crying out loud! But He does expect you to work hard to live your best life.

Now the word "best" is relative. My best is not your best, and your best is not your BFF's best. We are all in different places in our Christian journey and your journey is tailor made just for you. If you're a virgin, that means you're sexually pure, but that doesn't mean your mind, heart, and body are pure. You can be a virgin and still dress like a hoochie, sing nasty songs and fantasize about sex all day long. Ain't nothin' about that pure! So just know that there's more to purity than being a virgin.

So, what does God say about purity? Let's find out. Grab your Bible and open it to 1 Corinthians 6:19-20. Don't have a Bible? No problem. Grab your phone. I know you've got one of those. Go to the app store and search Bible. There are several Bible apps out there, but my personal favorite is YouVersion. Download it for free and use it bookmark the verses that you want to go back to later. Let's read:

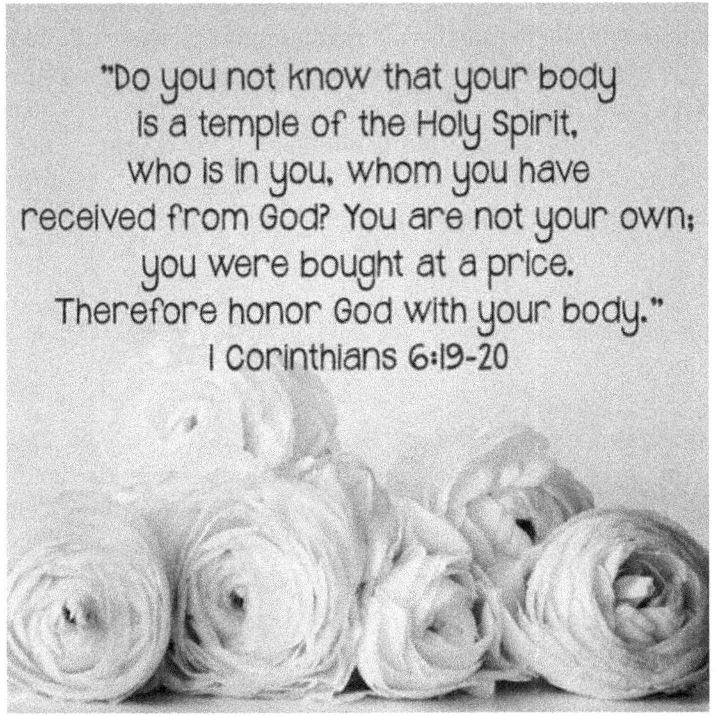

Let's break this down piece by piece.

"Do you not know that your body is a temple of the Holy Spirit, who is in you, whom you have received from God?"

What do you think this means? A temple is a building of worship and the Holy Spirit is the guiding voice of God that helps you make decisions. God sent us the Holy Spirit so that He can always be with us. It is the embodiment of God within us. Because God and the Holy Spirit live inside of us (the temple) then we shouldn't do anything to our bodies that will displease God. Let's take a look at the next part.

"You are not your own. You were bought at a price."

The price God paid for your life was the highest - the life of His son Jesus. Jesus paid the price of death so we could live. He made the ultimate sacrifice, so your sins would not separate you from God. So, think of your body, your mind and your soul, not as yours, but borrowed from God. How would you treat something that you borrowed from God? With the upmost care and respect, right? That's the way you should treat your body.

The last verse says.

"Therefore honor God with your body."

That sounds simple enough. But how does it apply in real life? How does it translate into what you actually do (and don't do) with your body? It all revolves around the word *honor.*

Honor means: *having high respect for and feeling privileged to be associated with someone.* So, if you honor God with your body, you should show respect for Him with the things you do with your body. You should do things that show you know it's a privilege to be His daughter. You should feel proud of the things you do with your body because God sees and approves.

Now, you're probably feeling one of two ways right now. Either extremely proud because you've been respecting God with your body, or a little bit guilty because you haven't. It's ok. If you're proud, there's always something you can do better and if you're embarrassed then you've definitely got some work to do.

Remember, purity permeates through everything we do. It's not just about sexuality. It seeps through our every thought and our every action. Take a look at a few things regarding purity. Ask yourself:

"How do I show purity in . . ."

The food I eat?
The beverages I drink?
The music I listen to?
The shows I watch?
The clothes I wear?
My relationships with boys?
The things I do with body?
The words I say?
The thoughts I have?

Think about how God wants you to show purity in everything you do. Why? Because the devil has a 24/7 campaign running to make you think purity is something to be ashamed of. I know that may sound strange, but think about it. When was the last time you saw or heard someone being celebrated for expressing their purity outside of church? Waiting . . . waiting . . . still waiting. Crickets. That's what I thought.

The world does not make it easy to tweet, post or even give someone else a shout out for living a life of purity. It's hard. It takes a lot of guts to unapologetically say you're not down for pre-marital sex, drinking, grinding, wearing skimpy clothes, and watching X-rated movies and videos. It's the right thing to do, but the world will tell you it's neither right nor wrong; just a matter of opinion.

The line between right and wrong has been blurred by people that don't want to feel guilty about their lifestyle. The guilt you feel is God's way of telling you that you need to change. The line between right and wrong is only blurred in the eyes of people. In God's eyes it's crystal clear!

2

Let's Talk About Sex

Alright girls, it's time to have a real honest conversation about sex. We're going to talk about things every girl needs to know in order to be fully equipped to emerge victorious in the battle for purity. Put on your big girl panties 'cause I'm keepin' it real!

The First Time Isn't Romantic - It Hurts

I know it's not what you were hoping to hear, but for most women, the first time is painful. No matter how many rose petals are on the bed or what music is playing in the background, losing your virginity is an uncomfortable experience. The hymen is a thin membrane of tissue that surrounds and narrows the vaginal opening. When women have sex for the first time this tissue is stretched and sometimes broken. Ouch! We're talking about stretching an area of the body that has never been stretched before, and a highly sensitive area at that. Sometimes the tissue may already be broken if you use tampons or play sports. But sometimes it isn't. That what causes the pain.

You Can Get Pregnant

You **can** get pregnant when having sex for the first time. The only requirement for pregnancy is the union of one sperm and one egg. Pregnancy can even happen if you haven't had your first period. Your body starts ovulating (producing eggs) 14 days before your period starts. That means your body is producing eggs before you see any signs of your period. You can also get pregnant during your period. Sperm can live in the body for up to 5 days, so if you ovulate within 7 days of having sex, you could get pregnant.

Dismiss all the stories about not getting pregnant while having sex standing up, in a pool or a hot tub. All myths. It's also a myth that you can't get pregnant if the guys *pulls out*. There's nothing that you can eat or drink after sex that will prevent pregnancy 100% of the time. Even the morning after pill is only 89% effective. A man can release 300,000 sperm during sex and it only takes one of them to get you pregnant. Don't risk it.

Guys Will Lie To Get Sex

I'm not trying to bash guys, but many of them will say whatever it takes to talk you into having sex. When their hormones are raging and their bodies are excited they want what they want. Period. So, no matter how reluctant you may be and regardless of any agreements you had about not having sex, they *will* persist. The most common words a guy will utter are "I love you," and "if you love me, you'll do it." You also may hear, "I'll be gentle," and "it'll just be this one time." Please know it won't be the last time he asks for sex and it only takes one time to lose your virginity. You can't make *your* decision based on what a guy says.

Oral Sex Is Sex Too

Despite the fact that many people don't classify oral sex as "real sex," it is. Countless studies and polls show that some girls still consider themselves virgins even after participating in oral sex. We won't debate that point here, but hear me when I say that sex is sex. Use 1 Corinthians 6: 19-20 as your measuring stick. Is giving or receiving oral sex honoring God with your body?

STDs Are No Joke

Anytime you have sexual contact, you're putting yourself at-risk for contracting a STD. The facts speak for themselves:

- Adolescents age 15-24 account for nearly half of the 20 million new cases of STD's each year
- Today, 4 in 10 sexually active teen girls have had an STD that can cause infertility and even death
- Males make up more than two-thirds of HIV diagnosis among 13-19 year olds.
- STDs often have no obvious signs or physical symptoms
- The most effective way to prevent an STD is to abstain from sexual activity
- Young people ages 15-24 have the highest rates of reported cases of chlamydia and gonorrhea

Soul Ties

A picture is worth a thousand words and this one expresses sexual soul ties perfectly. Sexual soul ties are bonds that develop between two people when they have sex. What do you see in the image below?

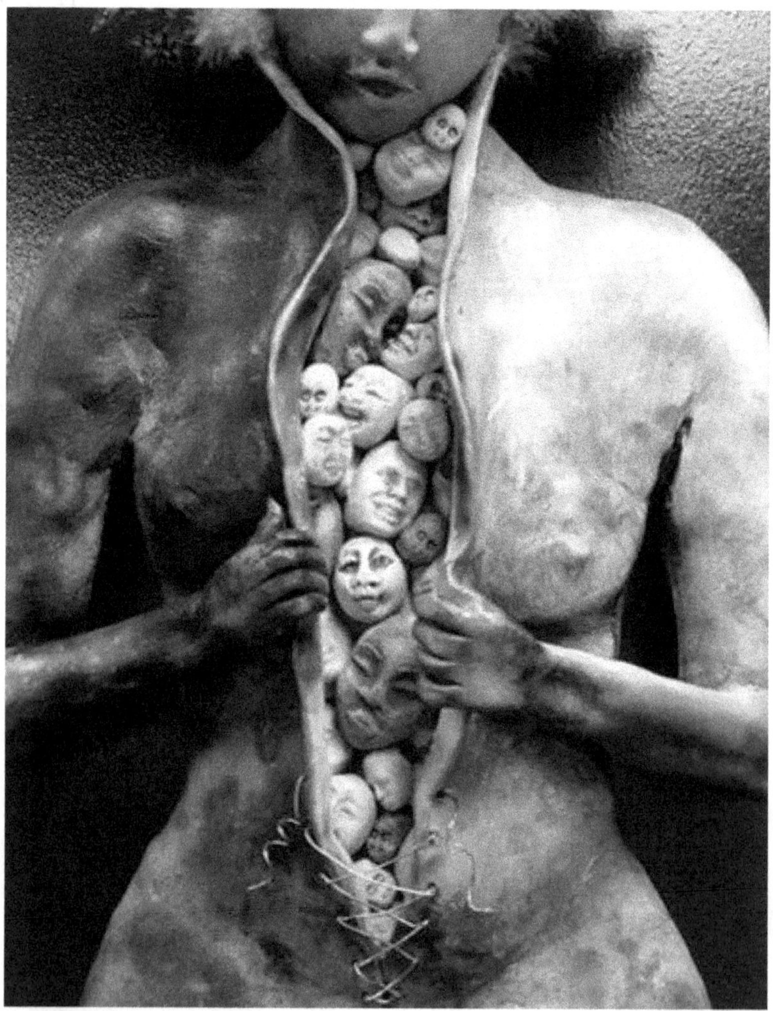

Self Discovery by Kim Reyes

Sex Creates Soul Ties

Sex at a young age can be a dangerous, damaging experience. For girls, sex brings about powerful emotions. Each time you engage in sex with someone, you become forever bonded with that person. It's not just a physical act but an emotional, mental, and spiritual act as well. Sex in the Bible is described as "becoming one flesh." In fact, one of the Greek words for joined also means "glued to." Whenever two things are glued together, it's impossible to separate them without doing some damage to one or the other. Just like the woman in the sculpture, the people you have sex with are bonded with you. When you separate, there will be damage.

Don't Experiment

It's perfectly normal to be curious about sex, but curiosity can get you into a situation that you'll later regret. Using the internet to explore sex will take you to pornographic websites that can become addictive. What may start as curiosity can lead to spending more and more time looking at pornography. Once porn images and videos are in your head, you begin to replay them in your mind. Left unchecked, this can lead to a desire to act out what you see. Worst of all, it can lead to porn addiction.

Experimenting with sexual acts with girls, oral sex and group sex can also become addicting and lead to thoughts of homosexuality and bi-sexuality.

Male vs Female. Your Body Doesn't Know the Difference.

Don't interpret being aroused by female body parts or being touched intimately by a girl as a sign you're a lesbian. The human body doesn't know the difference between a touch from a male and a touch from a female. Think of it like this. If you were blindfolded and touched intimately by a female and then by a male, your body would react exactly the same. It's basic human anatomy. The body physically reacts to certain types of stimulation. Don't get it twisted. Just because your body responds to a girl doesn't mean you're gay!

Pre-marital Sex Can Cause Trouble for Your Future Marriage

You don't need to drag any unnecessary baggage into your future marriage and that's exactly what pre-marital sex is- baggage. The last thing you want are memories of past boyfriends creeping into your mind when you're a married woman.

Sex is a Beautiful Blessing - for Married Folks

I'm not trying to scare you into thinking sex is some horrific experience. It's a beautiful, intimate experience that God created for a husband and wife to share. It only gets scary and confusing when unmarried people put it into practice. All things operate in excellence when they unfold according to God's plan. Sex is no different.

3
Abstinence – It is Possible!

Abstinence is possible, but boy is it hard! I'm not trying to discourage you, but if abstinence is the choice you're going to make (and it's the right one) you have to know what lies ahead. And just so you know, if you've already lost your virginity, you *can* re-commit yourself to being abstinent.

The abstinence road can be a bumpy one, but it's not impossible to stay on. What makes it difficult to navigate are all the seductive side streets, racy off ramps and devious detours. The road hasn't always been quite so dangerous. Potholes have always been there, but now it's also littered with messages that tell you that premarital sex is okay. You get them from advertisements, television shows, movies, music and social media. Sure, you still have family, friends and the church to encourage you to wait, but the media is a giant in the world of influence that cannot be ignored. Just like the giant Goliath, it can be defeated if you know *how* to fight. In order to emerge victorious in the battle to stay abstinent, you have to decide for yourself that **IT IS POSSIBLE**!

If you go into a fight believing you can't win, you won't. Being abstinent is no different. The first part of the decision is being clear about what abstinence means. The textbook definition of abstinence is *the practice of not doing something.* That something in this case is sex. The decision to practice sexual abstinence is the decision **not** to have sex.

So how do you define sex? Do you think sex includes intimate touching, tongue kissing or making out? Do you think it includes oral sex or just "traditional sex?" This question has been debated over and over and will continue to be debated until the end of time. For this discussion, we'll define sex as: *the touching of any intimate body parts to include the penis, breasts, vagina and buttocks.* Sorry to be so formal, but we have to make sure we're on the same page here. In order for you to have a clear idea of the commitment you're making to God about sexual abstinence, you have to come up with your own definition of sex. Think about it and when you're ready write it here.

My definition of sex:

____

____

____

____

Now, back to the decision. There are several parts to making this decision. I could just tell you about them, but I'd rather you hear it from teens who are actually doing it. Go to my website, write4queenz.com, and hover over the Royal Resources tab. Click videos. Watch the video entitled *The Decision to be Abstinent.* As you watch, fill in the blanks on the worksheet on the next page. We'll reconnect in a few minutes!

Making the Decision

Go to write4queenz.com, click on Royal Resources and watch video #1: *Making the Decision.* Fill in the blanks as you watch. Answers on the next page. No peeking! ☺

1. The first sign of growth is __________.

2. __________ can make the decision **not** to be sexually available.

3. Having pre-marital sex wasn't going to help me be __________ okay.

4. The emotional consequences of sex are __________.

5. Each _______, each ______ takes away a piece of you.

Here are the main points from the video:

1. The first sign of growth is change.
2. Everybody can make the decision **not** to be sexually available.
3. Having pre-marital sex wasn't going to help me be emotionally okay.
4. The emotional consequences of sex are overwhelming.
5. Each partner, each time takes away a piece of you.

So, what do you think? The message is pretty clear. Abstinence is a decision that anybody can make, but only you can make that decision for yourself.

Making the Decision

So, are you ready to make the abstinence decision? Maybe you've made it in the past, but gave in to temptation. It's not too late. You can start over. You may be saying to yourself, well it's easy to *say* you're not going to have sex but how do you actually not do it? The first step is telling God about it. Don't just tell God you're going to try not to have sex. The word try creates a loophole – a way out of sticking to your decision. Just say, "God, I'm not having sex." It makes the decision more real, more serious. The second step is to ask God to help you. Then, tell someone you trust and ask them to help you live your decision. You need someone to encourage you and hold you accountable.

Ready? All you have to say is, "God, I'm going to be sexually abstinent. Help me live my decision."

Living the Decision

The young people in the first video did a great job sharing how they made the decision to be abstinent. Now, you'll get to hear *how* they are making it happen. On next page, circle the words you think complete the sentences. Then go to write4queenz.com, hover over the Royal Resources link and click Videos. Watch video #2: *Living the Decision.*

Living the Decision

Circle the answers that complete the sentences below. Then, go to write4queenz.com, hover over the Royal Resources link and click Videos. Watch video #2: *Living the Decision.*

1. If the person loves you they will:
   a) talk you into having sex
   b) wait
   c) break up with you

2. The decision to <u>remain</u> abstinent is:
   a) easy
   b) crazy
   c) hard

3. For women, sex is very:
   a) physical
   b) traumatic
   c) emotional

4. The first rule of abstinence is to have:
   a) condoms
   b) boundaries
   c) no boyfriend

5. It's easier to be abstinent with a:
   a) parent present
   b) enemy's curse
   c) friend's help

Here are the answers from the video.

#1. If the person loves you, they will *__wait.__* Plain and simple. Sex is not a prerequisite for love. One can certainly exist without the other.

#2 The decision to remain abstinent is *__hard.__*
They key word is *remain*. The ultimate goal is for you stay abstinent until you get married and that's not an easy task. It's human nature to desire intimacy with another person, so don't ever feel guilty about that. Just press pause on acting on those feelings until you say "I do."

#3 For women, sex is every *__emotional.__*
Women often become emotionally attached after having sex. Guys, not so much. You can be left feeling confused and hurt after sex. Especially if the guy ends the relationship.

#4 The first rule of abstinence is to have *__boundaries.__*
Boundaries, boundaries, boundaries! You have to set boundaries early in relationships. Let guys know that you are abstinent and you are going to stay that way. Don't allow yourself to be in a situation where you're alone with a guy. Never being alone makes it pretty hard to have sex.

#5 It's easier to remain abstinent with a *__friend's help.__*
Friends hold each other accountable. Like the girl in the video said, if you find yourself in a sticky situation, a friend can help remind you of your commitment and talk you out of doing something you'll regret later.

So, we've talked about making the decision to be sexually abstinent and about living the decision to be abstinent. Now let's talk about the advantages of being abstinent. Yes, there are advantages! The most obvious advantage is knowing you're following the Word of God by saving sex for marriage. But there are plenty of other advantages that go along with it.

When you live a life of abstinence, you have no worries about pregnancy or STDs. You also don't have to worry about the emotional soul ties that come along with sexual partners. Going into a relationship without the baggage and distractions of previous sexual partners is a huge advantage.

The last part of this video series is called *Advantages of the Decision.* Go to write4queenz.com, hover over the Royal Resources link and click Videos. Take a look at video #3. You'll find the main points on the next page.

Advantages of the Decision

1. More time to work on yourself.

2. Peace of mind, which is priceless!

The last thing I will share with you in this chapter are letters from teenage girls. These are excerpts from real letters written by teen girls that decided to have sex before marriage.

Letters from Teenage Girls

"Premarital sex gave me fear as a gift and shame to wear as a garment. It stole my peace of mind and robbed me of hope and a bright future . . ."

"Sex killed my concentration in school. My desire for church was ground to a pulp. It made crumbs of the trust I had in Christ. Sex gave me a jagged tear in my heart that seven years later is still healing."

"I'm 13 and I just ruined my life. I thought Mike really loved me. Last night we had sex for the 1st time and he has now told me he doesn't want to see me anymore. I thought giving him what he wanted would make him happy. What if I'm pregnant? What am I going to do? I feel so alone and confused. I don't know how I can go on."

"Having sex was the most horrifying experience I've ever had in my life. It wasn't at all the emotionally satisfying or the casually taken experience the world perceives it to be. I felt as if my insides were being exposed and my heart left unattended."

If you've already had sex and were writing a letter about how you felt afterwards, what would you say?

4

Temptation: How to Find the Escape Route

The only temptations that you have are the same temptations that all people have. But you can trust God. He will not let you be tempted more than you can bear. But when you are tempted, God will also give you a way to escape that temptation. Then you will be able to endure it.
1 Corinthians 10:13

When I talk about temptation, I like to use the analogy of a fire escape. A fire escape provides a way for you to escape from a dangerous situation. It's not the route that we would normally use to get out of a building, but when our regular way is blocked by fire or smoke, we use the fire escape to take us to safety. In this chapter I'm going to tell you how God is like a fire escape.

Fire Escapes Are Strong

Fire escapes are made of iron or steel and can support a lot of weight. That's important because in an emergency, everybody heads to the fire escape. Nobody concerns themselves about how much weight the stairs can support. Unlike an elevator that has a weight limit, stairs do not. This is just like God. No matter how big and heavy the temptation may be, it's not too heavy for God. He can handle it and deliver us safely out of the situation no matter how hard it may be.

Fire Escapes Are Clearly Marked.

You can always recognize the glowing red exit sign that sits above every stairwell exit. It's pretty hard to miss. All buildings are required to post maps that show emergency escape routes. They want to make it quick and easy for people to leave the building in an emergency.

When you find yourself in an emergency (tempting situation) God makes the escape route clear. He always provides a way out of situations that lead to sin. You may not recognize the way out at first, but the harder you look, the easier it will be to find. It takes practice to learn how to identify the exit signs. Take a look at this example.

Last week a pop up porn ad appeared on Sarah's cell phone. She clicked on it and has spent the last three days, on porn sites watching X-rated videos. After watching, she feels guilty and prays to God to help her stop.

The next time Sarah picks up her phone another pop up appears. She starts to click on the website, but her mother comes into her room and asks her to get the groceries out of the car. When she comes back to her room, her phone battery is dead. She plugs it into the charger, and when the battery is full, another pop us ad appears. Sarah click on it, but gets a message that the website cannot be found.

In this example, God provided Sarah three opportunities to escape the temptation of pornography. The first was her mother asking for help with the groceries. The second was her phone battery dying and the third was the website error message. There were no claps of thunder or lightning strikes in the sky, but each situation provided an opportunity for Sarah to escape the video. This is what God does. He provides opportunities for you to escape temptation, but you have to actually take the route.

Fire Escapes Require Work

Hop on an elevator, push a button and you arrive at your destination in seconds. Fire escapes are different. They require some work on your part. To get to your destination, you have to be willing to do some work.

God will provide the route, but you have to make the decision to use it. You must climb out of the situation. Just like in a fire, you have to make the decision to escape fast. You don't have time to think about whether or not you should leave. The fire is getting hotter, spreading fast and consuming everything in its path – just like temptation. The longer you stay in a tempting situation, the more difficult it is to get out of. Temptation is like a magnet, it draws you in. The closer you get to it, the stronger the attraction.

No matter what kind of physical shape you're in, climbing stairs is tiring. Walking away from temptation is hard work. No matter the issue. When we're faced with temptation our minds and spirits are at battle. We have to work hard to make a quick decision to run to the fire escape and climb to safety in order to win.

God and fire escapes are similar, but there is one important difference. Everyone can recognize a fire escape, but only some people can recognize an escape route in a moment of temptation. You may see an escape route as just a coincidence or as an obstacle standing in the way of what you want. In reality, it's protecting you from something you'll regret. How do you learn to recognize the escape route? Study the Word and talk to God.

Check out the staircase on the next page to learn about four steps that will help you avoid temptation and find the escape route.

Four Steps to Avoid Temptation

Recognize the Way Out

My sheep listen to my voice. I know them, and they follow me. John 10:27

Look for the Escape Route

But when you are tempted, God will also give you a way to escape that temptation. Then you will be able to endure it. 1 Corinthians 10:13 ERV

Avoid What Tempts You

Watch and pray so that you will not fall into temptation. The spirit is willing, but the flesh is weak." Matthew 26:41

Know What Tempts You

Everyone ought to examine themselves. . . 1 Corinthians 11:28 NIV
You are tempted by the evil things you want. Your own desire leads you away and traps you. James 1:14 ERV

Step 1: Know What Tempts You

Be brutally honest with yourself about the things that tempt you that are not God's will.

> *Everyone ought to examine themselves 1 Corinthians 11:28 NIV*
> *You are tempted by the evil things you want. Your own desire leads you away and traps you. James 1:14 ERV*

No one else has to know, but you have to recognize what temps you so you know how to deal with it. It may be pornography, it may be sex, it may be alcohol. Whatever it is, God already knows, so recognize it and deal with it.

Step 2: Avoid Temptation

Don't fool yourself into thinking you're stronger than you are.

> *Watch and pray so that you will not fall into temptation. The spirit is willing, but the flesh is weak." Matthew 26:41.*

Temptation is strong, but temptation alone is not a sin. Even Jesus was tempted by Satan in the wilderness:

Then Jesus was led by the Spirit into the wilderness to be tempted by the devil. After fasting forty days and forty nights, he was hungry. The tempter came to him and said, "If you are the Son of God, tell these stones to become bread."
Jesus answered, "It is written: 'Man shall not live on bread alone, but on every word that comes from the mouth of God.'"
Then the devil took him to the holy city and had him stand on the highest point of the temple. "If you are the Son of God," he said, "throw yourself down. For it is written:
"He will command his angels concerning you, and they will lift you up in their hands, so that you will not strike your foot against a stone.'"

Jesus answered him, 'It is also written: 'Do not put the Lord your God to the test.'"
Again, the devil took him to a very high mountain and showed him all the kingdoms of the world and their splendor. "All this I will give you," he said, "if you will bow down and worship me."
Jesus said to him, "Away from me, Satan! For it is written: 'Worship the Lord your God, and serve him only.'"
Then the devil left him, and angels came and attended him.
Matthew 4:1-11

Jesus didn't succumb to the three temptations offered by Satan. He was led into the wilderness specifically for this test by the Spirit. " . . . *Jesus was led by the Spirit into the wilderness to be tempted by the devil.*" But don't purposely put yourself in situations to test your strength against temptation. The consequences are too serious if you fail.

If you don't put yourself in situations where you will be tempted, you'll have a much better chance at avoiding it. Remember Sarah and the cell phone? What are some things she could do in the future to avoid that temptation? How about only using her cell phone around family members? That would certainly discourage her from pulling up porn videos. She could also block websites with mature ratings so they don't come up. Avoidance is not fail proof, but it certainly makes getting into a tempting situation more difficult.

Step 3: Look For the Escape Route

As soon as you realize you're facing temptation, start looking for a way out. Don't wait. Don't trick yourself into thinking you can handle it. The longer you stay in the situation, the harder it will be to get out. It's called temptation for a reason. IT'S TEMPTING! It's something your flesh wants.

"You are tempted by the evil things you want. Your own

> *desire leads you away and traps you. James 1:14 ERV*

Your escape route could be another person, a Word from God, or a literal "door" out of the situation. When the door opens, run like the devil himself is chasing you! Remember that God allows us to be tempted, but He never temps us. So, when something or someone is tempting you, the devil is orchestrating the situation. Whatever tempts you is going to look appealing, so don't let that distract you from the fact that it will lead to sin. God will send an escape route, but you have to take it.

Step 4: Recognize God's Voice

God's voice is the way out. God will speak to you and let you know you're in danger. But you have to be able to recognize His voice. How do you recognize it? The same way you recognize anyone else's voice. By hearing it over and over again. The more time you spend with God, the easier it will be to recognize his voice. Talk to Him, pray to Him and read His Word.

When Jesus was in the wilderness, He used the Word of God to defend Himself against the devil's attack.

> *Jesus answered, "It is written: 'Man shall not live on bread alone, but on every word that comes from the mouth of God' . . . It is also written: 'Do not put the Lord your God to the test . . . For it is written: 'Worship the Lord your God, and serve him only.' Matthew 4: 4, 7, 10.*

It took me a long time to start recognizing God's voice. Whenever I was tempted to do something I shouldn't, I would hear a voice whispering, "Danger, danger." I thought it was my conscious. I didn't realize until later that it was God. Now, not only can I recognize God's voice in a tempting situation, I can hear Him warning me *before* I get myself into it. Keep talking to God and you'll hear Him warning you too.

Another way to recognize God's voice is through prayer. Pray every day and talk to God on a regular basis. You don't have to use fancy words, just tell Him what's on your mind. Soon, you'll be able to hear His voice as clear as day. Not only will you hear God, you will feel Him. God will warn you through your feelings. Pay close attention to those uneasy, uncomfortable feelings you get. Don't shrug them off. It's God's way of warning you about danger. The more you talk to God, the easier it will be for you to recognize temptation. Then you can fight temptation and win!

Nothing is *cute enough* to compensate for how modesty *feels.*

Unknown author

5
Modest Dress: Holy, Not Hoochie

This definition of modesty is more powerful than any other I've heard. N*othing* is cute enough to compensate for how modesty *feels*.

Sometimes when I'm getting dressed for work, I'll say to my husband "Do you think these pants are too tight?" or "Do you think this skirt is too short?" He always says the same thing. "If you have to ask me, then you don't need to wear it." He's right. If I'm asking, that means I'm already feeling *some kind of way* about how I look in it. That's God's way of saying, "Sweetheart, you need to change."

The way you dress has an impact on how you see yourself, how others see you. Modest dress gives you an inner beauty that comes across to others as calm confidence. Have you ever thought about why dress the way you do? How you decide which pieces of clothing grace your body and which ones don't? Where do you draw the modesty line? It all depends on your definition of modesty. Write your definition of modesty here.

Modesty is ____

____

Now, let's see what modesty looks like to you. On the next page you will find six pictures. Rate each picture on a scale of 1 to 5 based on your definition of modesty. A 5 is very modest, while a 1 is not modest at all. Then, put a check mark beside the outfits you would wear.

What Does Modesty Mean to You?

Girls, rank the following outfits from 1 to 5 with 1 being not modest at all and 5 being very modest. Put a check beside the outfits you would wear.

1 2 3 4 5
Not modest — Very modest

1 2 3 4 5
Not modest — Very modest

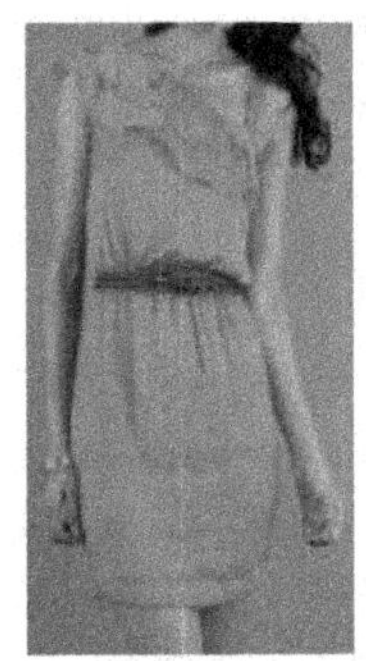

1 2 3 4 5
Not modest — Very modest

1 2 3 4 5
Not modest — Very modest

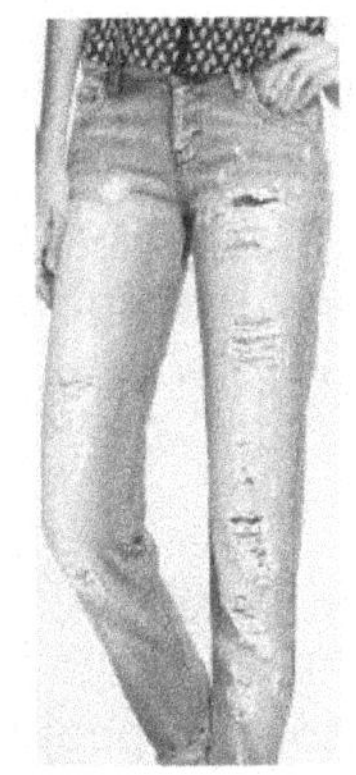

1 2 3 4 5
Not modest — Very modest

1 2 3 4 5
Not modest — Very modest

"*. . . likewise also that women should adorn themselves in respectable apparel, with modesty and self-control*"
1 Timothy 2:9

Girls, I encourage you to do this activity with a friend. Things become clearer when we talk to other people.
Go to write4queenz.com, hover over Royal Resources and click on the Modesty Quiz.

I hear a lot people say "You shouldn't judge a book by its cover." I agree, but we do it all the time. Imagine this. You know a girl you want to introduce to your cousin (he needs a date for the prom). She's nice and always dresses cute at school, but today she looks different. Her dress is super tight and so short you can almost see her underwear. All her cleavage is hanging out and she has on way too much make-up. Do you still introduce her to your cousin? Would the way she looks cause you to think twice? This new perception you have of her may not be accurate; nevertheless, it's your reality.

What we wear communicates messages to other people. Whether the message is accurate or not is irrelevant because a person's perception is their reality. People are going to treat you based on their perception of you, so if you want to be treated like a virtuous woman, you have to dress like one.

Virtuous women come in many different packages. You have to figure out what your package looks like. Are you happy with the perception other people have of you based on the way you dress? You may have to do a little research to answer that question. Think about the reaction you get when you go out. What kind of looks do you get? Do people make comments? Ask someone you trust to give you their honest opinion. Spend some time thinking about what they say. If you're still having trouble, take a look at girls that dress similar to the way you do. What's your opinion of them? Most importantly, pay attention to what God is telling you about the way you dress. Pray and He will answer.

Time for another video! Jerry (Jflo) and Tanisha Flowers host a series of videos on their Yoube Channel called Redefined TV. Take a look at their video on modest dress. Go to write4queenz.com, hover over the Royal Resources tab and click Videos. Watch video #4. J'Flo and Tanisha's have an interesting perspective on modest dress!

Here are the three main points in J'Flo and Tanisha's video.

1. The way you dress, advertises the way you view yourself.
2. The way you dress will dictate the way that you are *addressed.*
3. If you dress like a piece of meat, the dogs will come running.

Here are a few other points they make about modest dress.

◊ when you know your self-worth and value in Christ, there are some things you just won't wear
◊ you never misrepresent Christ at the expense of being trendy
◊ a daughter of the King, should never be confused with a woman of the night
◊ you represent a kingdom, not just you
◊ when you're getting dressed, ask yourself, is this something that represents Christ well?
◊ consider your brothers that are trying to be pure with the eyes
◊ you can't have a high standard and a low presentation
◊ a Godly man wants a woman that represents Christ
◊ don't use your body as bait to lure men

My husband once told me that girls don't dress for guys, girls dress to compete with other girls. I see his point. Sometimes you do have guys in mind when you're shopping for clothes or getting dressed. It's natural to want guys to find you attractive. There is a cloud of competition that exist among women that perpetuates the feeling that you have to look better than the next girl to get the guy. This competition is heavily influenced by the media. I'll talk more about that in chapter 7. Just know that a Godly man wants a virtuous woman, and to be virtuous, you must look the part.

Before I end this chapter, I encourage you to explore other videos on modest dress on my website like, *A Christian Guys Plea* and *The Modesty Series.*

6
Choosing Friends (and Boyfriends)

If I've heard it once, I've heard it a thousand times, "You don't need a whole lot of friends, just a faithful few." My mom used to say those words to me all the time when I was a teenager. But like most teens, I wanted to have lots of friends. It didn't work out that way. There were lots of people that I wanted in my friendship circle that just didn't fit. Or maybe it was *me* that didn't fit into *their* circle. Either way, we didn't connect. But it wasn't a bad thing. Mom was right. I didn't have a whole lot of friends, but I had a small circle of really good ones. I think I was better off for it.

When I think about why some people didn't fit into my circle, I keep coming back to the same two things: lifestyle and beliefs. As a teen, your lifestyle and your beliefs are forever evolving. At this stage in your life you begin to form your identity. You start discovering who you are and what you believe in. Your ideas about God, family, friends, relationships and life in general will change over and over again. That's not a bad thing. Exploring new ideas and experiencing different things is the only way you'll find out what you like and what you don't like.

Exploring the kind of people you like to be around, the places you like to go and the things you like to do, helps you define who you are.

Some of the most important things in your life will happen with friends, so it's important that you choose them wisely. I compare choosing friends to cooking eggs. Yep, I said eggs. I know it sounds strange, but hang with me for a few minutes and I'll explain.

You've heard of the phrase "unequally yoked" right? It goes like this:

> "*You are not the same as those who don't believe. So don't join yourselves to them. Good and evil don't belong together. Light and darkness cannot share the same room.*"
> 1 Corinthians 6:14.

I always thought this verse was referring to marriage, but the more I studied it, I realized that it applies to all relationships. God gives us awesome advice here about how to choose friends.

Did you know that Americans eat 76.5 billion eggs per year? That's a whole lot of unborn chickens we're digesting! Even though I have developed a dislike for eggs over the past few years (they make me want to puke), I can see why they're so popular. They're cheap, easy to make and can be used in lots of recipes. But I never thought of using them to describe friendships until God dropped this in my spirit.

When we meet new people, we treat the relationship like cooking eggs. We can boil eggs or we can scramble them. They're two very different processes.

When you boil an egg instead of scrambling it, you've

made the choice to invest more time cooking process. It takes about 10 minutes to boil an egg but only 2-3 minutes to scramble one. When you boil eggs you leave the shells on. The shell protects the delicate inside of the egg from the scalding hot water. It also provides a mold for the egg to solidify in as it hardens. The liquid, runny yolk changes into a solid. The yolk and whites are separate and cannot be mixed together.

Now let's relate that to a friendship. When you take your time and get to know someone, you give yourself protection from being damaged by that person. That time is like a wall. It allows you to get to know the real them, before you decide to let the wall down and build a relationship. That wall is your shell.

People show you their best side when you first meet them. They only let you see what they want you to see. So, don't let them get to close too soon. If you decide to peel off your shell later, that's fine. You've had some time to get to know them behind a layer of safety first. Stay in your shell and decide if the person is someone you want to be friends with or not. Don't put your feelings out there too soon and become vulnerable or your eggs may just get burned!

When you're solid on the inside (secure about who you are in relationship) you give yourself the option of ending the relationship with less stress and less damage. Think about it. If you throw two boiled eggs in a bowl and later decide you want to take one out, you can. Even if you chop them up, you can still take out the pieces. Not the case with scrambled eggs. Once they are together, there's no taking them apart. Give yourself time to get to know someone before diving in. If things don't work out, you can end the relationship before you get too emotionally attached.

God doesn't want you to get all scrambled up with people before you know what their intentions are. Don't crack open your shell right from the start. You may discover that their beliefs and lifestyle are not in line with yours. It's okay to make friends that are different, but it's not okay to make friends that pull you away from God. You can still show respect and care for people that make bad choices but 1 Corinthians 15:33 says, "*Bad friends will ruin good habits.*"

Sometimes God will bring people into your life so you can be an example for them. If you're too busy acting like a snobby Christian to develop a relationship with them, they may not get to know Christ. Now I said develop a relationship, not become BFFs. God doesn't want you to be unequally yoked. Remember the light and darkness? You can be anyone's acquaintance, but save your friendships for those you can grow with in Christ.

I can't end this chapter without giving you one more tool. It's an amazing video created by Darious Daniels, the Senior Pastor of Kingdom Church in Ewing Township, NJ. Pastor Daniels was a guest on a webisode of Redefined TV called *Boundaries: Indicators of an Unhealthy Relationship.* Go to write4queenz.com, hover over the Royal Resources link and click on videos. Watch video #5. Use the organizer on the next page to organize the important points.

Boundaries: Indicators of an Unhealthy Relationship

by Darious Daniels
Senior Pastor, Kingdom Church, Ewing Township, NJ

3 Questions to Ask Yourself

Does the relationship add value to my life or decrease my assets? *There are no neutral relationships. People either add value to your life, or they take it away*	
Does the relationship make withdrawals only, or does it make withdrawals and deposits? *If there are only withdrawals and no deposits, that's not a partner, it's a parasite!*	
Does the relationship help me bury or resurrect parts of me that I need to keep in the grave? *Proverbs 13:20 Walk with the wise and become wise, for a companion of fools suffers harm. You don't have to be a fool to suffer harm, just hang out with them.*	

7
The 5 Lies the Media Wants You to Believe

Did you know that Americans spend an average of 15.5 hours a day engaged in some type of media? That's 65% of our day watching videos, TV, on social media or listening to music. For 8 to 18 year olds, it's 7.5 hours a day, 7 days a week. That's more time than you spend sleeping!

You're probably thinking, "I know I spend a lot of time on my phone. Everybody does. What's the big deal?" The big deal is *what* are you being exposed to, *who's* exposing it to you and *why*? The media is the *who*. The *what* is a bunch of lies, and the *why* is to make money.

The media spends billions of dollars creating images and sounds that capture your attention. Their ultimate goal is not to make you laugh, cry or think, but to get you to spend money. TV, movies, and music companies all have to make money to exist. They make money by selling ideas. Every time you buy something, you're not just buying a product, you're buying an idea.

Here's a personal example. I am a faithful user of Mary Kay's Cosmetics liquid foundation. It's the only foundation I've used for the past 14 years. When I bought that first little white tube with the signature pink cap, I was buying the idea that this foundation would make me beautiful. I was buying the idea that I needed to cover up my skin's imperfections so I could appear flawless and be accepted by others. Now, of course that's not what the Mary Kay Consultant told me and it certainly isn't what I was thinking at the time I purchased it. But flawlessness is idea behind cosmetic ads.

Flawlessness is the biggest lie the media tries to sell you. It's the foundation of a multi-billion dollar beauty product industry. There's nothing wrong with buying and using beauty products. The problem is allowing a product, or the idea behind the product rule to your thinking.

Do you think you're beautiful? Can you answer that question without comparing yourself to some image you've seen in a magazine or video? Can you answer that question without imagining yourself all dolled up in a cute outfit with your hair done, nails done, and made up? It can be hard.

When I ask myself, "Am I beautiful?" two images pop into my head. The first image is me au' natural– no make-up, a ponytail, a pair of jeans and T-shirt. The second image is divalicious me. Fly outfit, cute heels, a French manicure, fabulous make-up and a fly hair-do. Which do I prefer? Quite honestly, the first is so much easier. It's easier (and more comfortable) not to worry about make-up, French nails, expensive hair dos and killer heels! So why do I spend all the time and money on the make-up, hair dos, nails, and cute clothes? Because they make me *feel* beautiful!

Have I been caught in the media's trap? Unfortunately at times, yes I have. It's impossible not to be effected by media when you're bombarded by ads day in and day out, every single day of your life. Their messages can have a powerful impact, but they don't have to *control* you. I don't let the media control my ideas or my beliefs. I know how to live in a media-saturated world that's rooted in money instead of values without letting it control me and you can too. If you buy these products, understand that they only impact the way you look, not who you are.

Everything you see with your eyes and hear with your ears is absorbed into your mind, subconscious and spirit. Those messages tell you who you are and what you should be like. All this media frenzy is not a coincidence, it's very much on purpose. Remember, the ultimate goal of the media is to sell products and make money. They want to convince you that whatever they're selling can buy you beauty, self-esteem and self-worth. I assure you it can't. But what it can do is fill your mind with images and messages about yourself that are damaging and just plain not true.

Flawlessness if just one of the lies the media tries to sell you. There are four more out there that are just as powerful and just as dangerous. I devoted a chapter to each one of them to explain how they work, and how you can conquer them.

8
Lie # 1: You Can Be Flawless

Walk down the beauty aisles of any drug store and you'll see just how much money is invested in beauty products. The average woman spends about $215 a year on make-up alone. That's $15,000 over a lifetime! That's a lot of mascara! I've spent my fair share of dollars on concealers, foundation, lipstick and eyeliner myself. But why?

The truth is these products make us feel beautiful so we buy them. Now don't start feeling guilty about wearing make-up. There's nothing wrong with it as long as you don't let the make-up control you. If you skip exercising, sleep-overs, or going to the pool because you're worried about messing up your hair or make-up, you're letting the products control you. Don't let the make-up control you. It's time to take a step back and assess your situation.

Do you ever go out with make-up on or your hair done? If not, your products have too much control. Try going out natural to prove to yourself that no one will stop and stare at you like you're an alien! The more you do it, the more control you gain.

For some of us, the quest for beauty goes beyond what we put on. Some women want a permanent change. In 2014, 13.6 million cosmetic procedures were performed on women that opted for plastic surgery. Over 200,000 of those procedures were performed on girls ages 13-19. That's almost a quarter of a million surgeries!

Have you ever imagined yourself with larger breasts, a thinner waist, fuller lips or more narrow hips? I know I have. A few years ago, I actually considered getting breast implants. Pregnancy had not been kind to "the girls" and I was feeling a bit self-conscious about my breasts. I researched plastic surgeons and even scheduled a consultation, but I ended up cancelling the appointment. I wish I could tell you that I had some revelation that I was just fine the way I was, but ultimately the fear of surgery changed my mind. I could never forgive myself if I ruined my good health or even lost my life for the chance to fill up a C cup. It just wasn't worth the risk; but for many girls and women, it is.

If you've thought about plastic surgery or had work done already, don't feel guilty. All women want to feel beautiful. We just take different journeys to try and get to that feeling. Just know that big boobs and a small waist don't make you beautiful. Beauty is in the eye of the beholder and the world's definition of beauty changes all the time. One day dark skin is in, the next it's light. One day relaxed hair is hot, the next day natural hair is all the rage. Don't adjust yourself to fit anyone else's definition of beauty. You must define beauty for yourself.

Jane Kilbourne is an author, speaker and activist who created an award winning project that exposes the damaging effects that advertisements and the media have on women. Kilbourne does an amazing job helping us see past the pretty images and into the messages behind the ads. Go to write4queenz.com, hover over Royal Resources tab and click on videos. Watch video #5.

That video really makes you think doesn't it? I know I'll never look at another ad the same way again. Here are some facts Jane Kilbourne shares about ads:

- ◊ ads sell normalcy (worldly definition of normal)
- ◊ ads tell us who we are and who we should be
- ◊ ads tell women that the most important thing is how we look
- ◊ ads make us feel ashamed and guilty when we don't attain ideal beauty
- ◊ no one looks like the ideal image in ads – not even the women in the ads
- ◊ women in ads are photo-shopped (reimaged by computer software) to perfection
- ◊ you almost never see an ad with a woman that has not been photo-shopped

So ladies, the point is you cannot be flawless because nobody's perfect! The Bible speaks about a woman's beauty and it is quite clear that our focus should not be on external beauty.

> *Do not let your adorning be external—the braiding of hair and the putting on of gold jewelry, or the clothing you wear— but let your adorning be the hidden person of the heart with the imperishable beauty of a gentle and quiet spirit, which in God's sight is very precious.* 1 Peter 3-4
>
> *Charm is deceitful and beauty is vain, But a woman who fears the LORD, she shall be praised.* Proverbs 31:30
>
> *As a ring of gold in a swine's snout. So is a beautiful woman who lacks discretion.* Proverbs 11:22

There are a few other videos on my website about beauty. To see the degree of editing ads go through check out video #7, *Models Without Make-Up*. Video #8, *You Can Be Flawless with Adobe by Photoshop*, shows you the industry's #1 secret to flawless beauty. For a little help appreciating your own natural beauty, check out video #9, *Try* by Colbi Callet.

Lie# 1: You Can Be Flawless
Truth: Nobody's Perfect

9
Lie # 2: Marriage Doesn't Matter

In 1960, 72% of adults ages 18 and older were married. Today, only 51% are married. Why the sharp decline in marriages over the last 55 years? There are lots of issues that come into play when we talk about marriage, but they all come down to one thing: attitude.

Attitudes about marriage have changed dramatically over the last half century. Gone are the days when a young woman is expected to be married by her early twenties. Only 9% of women ages 18-24 were married in 2010 compared to 45% in 1960. Quite simply, women have more options now than they did then in the past. More women are pursuing college and career training and focusing more on preparing themselves for careers as opposed to marriage. Career goals, the high divorce rate and the superwoman mentality have many women thinking that they just don't *need* a man.

These attitudes have pushed more women to pursue higher education and entrepreneurship than ever before. About 71% of today's female high school graduates enroll in college compared to the 63% who enrolled in 1994. Between 1997 and 2014 the number of women-owned businesses in the US increased by 68%. That's 1.5 times the national average. All that education and business savvy takes time, energy and hard work. Many women are putting relationships on hold while they pursue career opportunities.

Career opportunities are not the only reason fewer women are tying the knot at a later age. Fear of divorce also plays a part. It's hard to ignore the fact that about 50% of marriages end in divorce. Knowing that your marriage has the same odds of success as a quarter landing on heads is not very encouraging. It can make even the most optimistic girl a little leery of walking down the aisle. Many women feel like they need a plan B in case things don't work out.

This brings us to the superwoman mentality. "I can take care of myself! I can take care of my kids! I can take care of everything without a man!" Women are some of the most resilient and resourceful creatures on the planet. When life's circumstances aren't kind to us, we rise to the occasion. When money is scarce, our energy is zapped and our self-esteem is wavering, we find a way to pick ourselves up and keep going. We are survivors. But God wants us to do more than just survive – He wants us to flourish!

So what on Earth do career success, divorce and the superwoman mentality have to do with the media? Everything. The media sells us on the idea that marriage doesn't matter and that's not what God tells us.

> *Then the LORD God made a woman from the rib he had taken out of the man, and he brought her to the man. The man said, "This is now bone of my bones and flesh of my flesh; she shall be called 'woman, ' for she was taken out of man." For this reason a man will leave his father and mother and be united to his* ***wife****, and they will become one flesh.* Genesis 2:22-24

God makes it clear to us from Genesis that marriage is

what He intended. Adam and Eve were God's first human creation. They were the model for His intentions for man and woman. When God saw that Adam was lonely, He took Adam's rib and created Eve, a help mate. The fact that God uses part of Adam to create Eve symbolizes the unbreakable bond that He intended a husband and wife to share. Marriage clearly matters to God, but has been trivialized by the media.

The high divorce rate is part of the reason that thousands of children are living in single parent households. Choice is also part of that reason. Many women make the choice to have and raise children without a husband. This choice has been accepted, applauded and even promoted by what we see in the media. Let's look at some celebrity examples to see how the media accomplishes this.

Nia Long and Jill Scott have a lot in common. They're both very talented. They both have successful careers. And they both have children and are not married. Now before anyone gets all huffy and starts defending single moms let me say that these women, like all others, have the right to do whatever they like. Let me also say that the fact these women are not married doesn't make them any less valuable in my eyes or in the eyes of God. But the fact that the media has applauded and put a spotlight on the fact they are not married is not okay. In fact, it's very deliberate and done for a specific purpose.

Nia Long and Jill Scott are both single moms but they became single mothers under very different circumstances.

If you check out the November, 2011 issue of Ebony magazine, you'll find Nia Long on the cover. She's nude and showing off her pregnant belly. In the article, she tells Ebony magazine *"I honestly asked God for this."* She goes on to recount a conversation that she had with her doctor. He told her it would be difficult to have a child at age 40, but Long and her boyfriend kept trying. A few months later, she was pregnant. This was the second child Long would have unmarried.

Less than a year later, Long appeared on the cover of Essence magazine with her two sons. The cover tag read, "Nia Long: Single Satisfied and Raising Her Boys." Inside, Long is quoted as saying, "Marriage is not a priority for me. I'm not saying I'll never do it; it's just not where we are as a family."
This was also posted on the Essence website.

To find out how God answered Nia Long's prayers and gave her a patient man, how she felt when her son got his first acting job –"we did the happy dance!"–how she finds balance as a working mom and what she does to feel sexy pick up the April 2014 issue of ESSENCE, on newsstands March 7th.

What do you think about this? Is what Nia Long says in line with what God wants for His daughters? Think about how her words impact people and how they're delivered through the lens of the media. Marriage is portrayed as unnecessary. It's portrayed as a casual choice that's optional for having sexual relationships and children.

Jill Scott and her son are featured on the cover of the May 2013 issue of Ebony magazine. She tells Ebony, *"That I-can-do-it-by-myself mentality is a lie. I'm sorry if I hurt anybody's feelings, but you cannot do it all by yourself. You need a village: some aunties, grandmoms, friends. I couldn't do this by myself and would be a fool to think I could."* I'm glad Jill Scott honestly shares that parenting is not a one woman job. But did you notice that there is no father or husband mentioned on her village list? Jill Scott was married at the time her son was conceived, but she and husband later divorced. Did the media minimize that detail on purpose?

The media are masters at blurring the lines between acceptance of people and approval of what they do. They know that Nia Long and Jill Scott have millions of fans. They know these women are strong and have worked hard to build successful careers. Unfortunately, they have linked these attributes together with the notion that marriage doesn't matter and is totally optional for having children.

No matter what you see in the media, be sure that you align the choices you make with the choices God would want you to make. 1 Corinthians 7:1 says:

> *"It is good for a man not to have sexual relations with a woman." But because of the temptation to sexual immorality, each man should have his own* **wife** *and each woman her own husband.*

The media minimalizes and sensationalizes the fact that women are having children without husbands. It takes sex to have a baby and this Bible verse tells us that sex should only take place inside marriage.

Magazines are not the only place we see the idea that marriage doesn't matter. We see it in books, movies, and TV shows as well. Have you heard of the 90 Day Rule? The 90 Day Rule is a vow to not have sex with a guy for 90 days after you begin dating him. The rule was made popular in comedian Steven Harvey's book *Act Like a Woman Think Like a Man.* In the book, Harvey compares sex to benefits that someone would earn on a new job.

Harvey says, *"When I worked at Ford Motor Company, they have a probation period. You have to be on the job 90 days in order for Ford Motor Company to release their benefit package to you. Why do women, who possess the greatest benefit of them all, why you passing on your benefits to a guy who has not been on the job for 90 days and has not proven to you that he's worthy of a benefit package?"*

So, how does this compare to the word of God? Well, if you're looking for a Bible verse that literally says, "Thou shalt not have sex before marriage," you won't find it. People argue that because no such verse exist, sex before marriage is okay. But, just because the Bible does not explicitly say it's wrong, doesn't mean it's right. The Bible is not a laundry list of do's and don'ts. God is speaking to you about how you should live and what you should do. In some cases He provides guidance about what you *shouldn't* do. This is the case with pre-marital sex. God also speaks volumes about what marriage is. When we put those things together, His message to us is clear. **Sex is for marriage!**

Here are some verses that will help you understand marriage.

> *But because of the temptation to sexual immorality, each man should have his own wife and each woman her own husband.* 1 Corinthians 7:2

Here, marriage is offered as a way to avoid sexual immorality. If each woman has her own husband, she should have sex with him and will not be tempted into sexual immorality.

> *Let* ***marriage*** *be held in honor among all, and let the marriage bed be undefiled, for God will judge the sexually immoral and adulterous.* Hebrews 13:4

This verse tells us that God will judge those that are sexually immoral. It also says that marriage is honored and the marriage bed is undefiled. Marriage is to be honored by all. What takes place in the bed of a married couple is undefiled which means clean or unsoiled.

> *Flee from sexual immorality. Every other sin a person commits is outside the body, but the sexually immoral person sins against his own body.* 1 Corinthians 6:18

Flee or run from sexual immorality. Stay away and don't do it. That's pretty plain and simple.

> *"If a man has sexual relations with a virgin who he is not engaged to, then he must pay her father the full amount necessary to marry her.* (Exodus 22:16

This verse gives you an if/then situation. If a man has sex with a women he's not engaged to, he must marry her. He must marry her because marriage is the only circumstance that sex is permissible.

Media outlets are chocked full of images that tell you marriage doesn't matter. Many TV shows poke fun at marriage and portray it as a punishment instead of the reward that God intended. Some show premarital sex between couples that are dating and even couples that just met. Single couples are shown living together, having children and living as if they are married. It's as if marriage doesn't matter.

Don't be tricked by the explanation that the people on TV are actors and the stories aren't real. Remember the media statistics. We are exposed to an average of 15.5 hours of media a day. When your brain is exposed to the same message over and over, that message sinks in. It's unavoidable. But being aware is half the battle. Be aware that the messages are there and that people spend lots of time and money trying to sell you those ideas. Be careful of what you watch. Ask yourself if it aligns with the Word of God.

If you choose not to get married, that's okay. It's totally your choice. But if you choose not to get married you can't live like you *are* married (having sex, living together, having children). Let the word of God be your guide for marriage, and leave the media out of it!

Lie #2: Marriage Doesn't Matter
Truth: God Honors Marriage

10
Lie #3: Homosexuality is Not a Sin

Over the years, homosexuality has gradually risen to the surface of society. There was a time when two guys or two girls holding hands or kissing elicited gaping mouths, raised eyebrows and an occasional "Lord have mercy!" Not anymore. We have been so saturated with the media's images of gay love and gay rights that many of us are desensitized to it. It has become a normal part of life that we have been forced to accept. Homosexuality has been in existence since Biblical times and it's not going to vanish. We can't make it go away, so we have to accept the fact that it exist. But we don't have to approve of it.

The media tries to blur the lines of homosexuality by putting the focus on three ideas. Idea one - being gay is in. Idea two - gay people have rights. Idea three – people can love whoever they choose. I agree with all three. But these ideas put the spotlight on popularity, civil rights and love, and take it off the fact that it's a sin.

> *You shall not lie with a male as one lies with a female; it is an abomination.* Leviticus 18:22

An abomination is defined in Webster's Dictionary as *a vile, shameful, or detestable action.* No question as to what God thinks here! The Bible not only tells us straight up how God feels about homosexuality, it discusses the punishment for participating in this sin.

> *Because people did those things, God left them and let them do the shameful things they wanted to do. Women stopped having natural sex with men and started having sex with other women. In the same way, men stopped having natural sex with women and began wanting each other all the time. Men did shameful things with other men, and in their bodies they received the punishment for those wrongs.* Romans 1:26-27

> *If a man has sexual relations with another man as with a woman, they have committed a terrible sin. They must be put to death. They are responsible for their own death.* Leviticus 20:13

So, how can the media and society portray something that is clearly a sin as acceptable? Because society and the media reflect the ways of the world and not the ways of God. The media tries to blur the lines of homosexuality.

Blurring the Lines of Homosexuality

Blur Tactic #1 - It's Popular

Not a day goes by when there isn't a newspaper article, TV story or social media post about homosexuality. Over the past three years advocacy groups and individuals have petitioned for gay marriage rights. Numerous court cases have been filed and legislation has been put in place to address this issue. The media coverage of gay rights has been monumental. The more the issue is brought to our attention, the more we talk about it. The more we talk about it, the more popular it becomes. Some say that the media is a reflection of society while others say the media shapes society. The media has such a long reach and powerful influence, that the way they deliver news has a tremendous impact on how you see things and what you believe.

The popularity of homosexuality has made its way into TV and cinema. Flip through the channels on TV and you're sure to find a sitcom or reality show with gay characters. In the 2014, there were 32 homosexual or bisexuals couples on prime time network TV shows. On cable there were 64. Chances are some of the TV shows you watch have homosexual characters. Seven of the top ten TV shows of 2014 had homosexual characters. Some say this presence simply reflects the state of society, but the homosexual population in America currently sits at 3.4%. Those numbers don't match. So, why the overrepresentation of homosexuals on TV? Simple. To make it more acceptable and gain approval.

The Gay and Lesbian Alliance Against Defamation (GLAAD) is an organization that works to accelerate the acceptance of homosexual and transgender individuals. One of its goals is to increase the number of positive portrayals of homosexuals in movies. Why do they want to accomplish this? Sarah Kate Ellis, the CEO and president of GLADD says their goal is *"To change the hearts and minds of Americans around LGBT people."* Well that doesn't sound all bad. I mean no group of people should be stereotyped, shunned or discriminated against. But this change of heart and mind goes beyond acceptance. Ellis goes on to say that kids who are struggling with "coming out" need to see more positive images of homosexuals couples because *"in order to be it, you need to see it."*

The idea that kids who are struggling with their sexual identity, should be exposed to images of homosexual couples to help them *be it* (homosexual) is absurd! Ladies, you are still forming your identity so its common and normal to wonder about your sexuality. Don't freak out if you have thoughts about experiences with girls. You are surrounded by those images, so those thoughts may pop into your mind. That doesn't mean you're a lesbian.

Now that homosexuality has gotten society's stamp of approval, more and women are "coming out." Actresses, singers, and community leaders are announcing to the world that they are gay. Don't be swayed by any woman's choice to be gay. You can still admire the accomplishments these women have made without approving of their lifestyle.

When the people we admire and respect advocate for things, we are more open to their ideas. For example, when a woman like Robyn Roberts announces she is a lesbian, it makes us stop and take notice. Our thought process goes like this: *"This woman is talented, intelligent and one of the best news reporters in the country. She's an anchor on the number one morning news show in America and a cancer survivor for goodness sake! I like her. I like her professionalism, her drive her spirit – she's an amazing person. And she's a lesbian, so maybe it's not so bad."*

It's easy to blur the lines between the person and the choices they make. Our admiration, respect and love for people can influence our ideas. When we identify with someone because they look like us, have the same background as us or are living the same dream we have for ourselves, we tend to be more forgiving of what they do. You can still respect, love and admire that person. You can still groove to their music, laugh at their jokes, and be inspired by their work. But when it comes to lifestyle choices, you have to ask yourself if what they choose is in line with what pleases God.

Blur Tactic #2 - Gay People Have Rights

When you have the right to do something, that means it's allowed. Someone or some institution has given you permission to do it. But along with those rights comes responsibility. The two go hand in hand. You have the right to free speech, but that doesn't make it right for you to curse someone out or spread gossip about them. You have the right to drive at 16, but that doesn't make it right for you to blow through stop signs and cut people off. At 21, you'll have the right to drink alcohol, but that doesn't make it okay to take tequila shots until you pass out! With rights come responsibilities.

So, do you have the right to be gay? Yes, you have the right. But that doesn't make it right.

> *All things are allowed," you say. But not all things are good. "All things are allowed." But some things don't help anyone.* 1 Corinthians 10:23

The Right to Marry

To say there has been a swarm of media attention on the issue of gay marriage is an understatement. The debate has been going on for decades and will continue to be just that, a debate. But where do you stand? On the surface it looks like a human rights issue, but when you examine it closely, it's an issue of definition.

What's your definition of marriage? Has it changed over time? Some say marriage is a union by God between two people that love each. Others believe it's a lawful union between two people that get a marriage license. For others, it's a contract that allows people to file taxes together, get health insurance and property when their spouse dies. Webster's Dictionary defines marriage like this:

marriage - *The state of being united to a person of the opposite sex as husband or wife in a consensual and contractual relationship recognized by law (2): the state of being united to a person of the same sex in a relationship like that of a traditional marriage*

When I read those definitions I am surprised by two things. First, that there is a second definition that includes same sex couples. The American Heritage Dictionary was the first to add the words "same sex" in 2000. The second surprise is that God is nowhere to be found in the first definition. I guess I shouldn't be surprised since dictionary definitions typically reflect the culture, but to see it in print is disheartening. Now, let's look at the Biblical definition of marriage.

God designed marriage for humanity. As first described in Genesis and later affirmed by Jesus, marriage is a God-ordained, covenant relationship between a man and a woman. This lifelong, sexually exclusive relationship brings children into the world and thus sustains the stewardship of the earth. Biblical marriage — marked by faithfulness, sacrificial love and joy — displays the relationship between God and his people. (NAE, 2012)

This definition embodies the spirit and holiness of marriage. It includes six ideas that are seen in Biblical references to marriage in the Bible.

1) **Marriage Honors God's Covenant Relationship**
   Wives, be willing to serve your husbands the same as the Lord. A husband is the head of his wife, just as Christ is the head of the church. Christ is the Savior of the church, which is his body. [24] *The church serves under Christ, so it is the same with you wives. You should be willing to serve your husbands in everything. Husbands, love your wives the same as Christ loved the church and gave his life for it.*
   Ephesians 5:22-25

2) **Marriage is Between Man and Woman**
That is why a man leaves his father and mother and is joined to his wife. In this way two people become one. Genesis 2:24

3) **Marriage is Life-long**
A woman should stay with her husband as long as he lives. 1 Corinthians 7:39
And a husband should not divorce his wife. 1 Corinthians 7:11

4) **Marriage is Honorable**
Marriage should be honored by everyone. Hebrews 13:4

5) **Marriage Requires Fidelity**
And every marriage should be kept pure between husband and wife. God will judge guilty those who commit sexual sins and adultery. Hebrews 13:4

6) **Marriage is a God-union**
And God said, 'That is why a man will leave his father and mother and be joined to his wife. And the two people will become one. So they are no longer two, but one. God has joined them together, so no one should separate them." Matthew 19: 5-6

So, ask yourself, "What is my definition of marriage? Is my definition of marriage the same as God's?"

Blur Tactic #3 - People Can Love Who They Choose

God loves everyone and wants you to do the same. But when feelings cause you to act in a way that displeases God, you have to stop. When love is coupled with lust, pre-marital sex or un-Godly desires, it's time for a change.

God put things in order to keep you out of harm's way. He communicates with you through the Bible, the Holy Spirit and other people. When you understand what God requires of you and you make the decision to follow Him, doing something against His Word is unacceptable. It doesn't magically become unappealing or not tempting, but it does become unacceptable. So if loving someone kicks off a series of events that are unacceptable to God, choose not to love.

Lie #3: Homosexuality is not a Sin
Truth: Homosexuality is a Sin

11
Lie#4: It's Just A Song

It's a boring, rainy Saturday and you're in a "meeh" mood. Suddenly your favorite song comes. Your face lights up, your head starts bopping and your heart starts pounding! The lyrics express how you feel, the music has you pumped and you're transported to another place. Music is very powerful. It has the ability to change your mood. They're not just a songs. Music effects your attitude and your beliefs.

Numerous studies have examined music and how it influences attitude and behavior. None have concluded that music can *make* you behave a certain way, but most have found that it can impact the way you think. Music that has lyrics about sex, alcohol use and violence have a profound effect on how you view these things. Just like commercials, TV shows and videos, music is another media outlet that bombards you with ideas and impacts your thoughts. In the midst of being entertained, you are being exposed to ideas about everything from money to success to happiness. You have to be able to recognize these messages and filter through them.

A study done in 2011 examined the top 20 songs on Billboard. It revealed that the most popular songs were full of sex, alcohol, drugs and explicit language. Of the top 20 songs, eleven mentioned sexual acts, nine had sex as an overall theme, nine referenced alcohol or drugs and seven of the 20 used explicit language. As I scanned through the list I was surprised to see songs I listened to all the time.

The number two song on the list is Party Rock. I like Party Rock. I thought it was just a song about dancing but when I googled the lyrics, I found this:

> *I'm running through these hoes like Drano*
> *I got that devilish flow rock and roll no halo*
> *. . . One more shot for us*
> *Another round*
> *Please fill up my cup*
> *Don't mess around*
> *We just wanna see*
> *You shake it now*
> *Now you home with me*
> *You're naked now*

I never noticed some of those words before. Seeing those lyrics made me wonder what other lyrics I missed in songs I liked in 2011.

Moves Like Jagger is a song my daughter listened to a lot. She thought it was about dancing, but I knew it was really about sex. I thought the sexual references were subtle until I read the lyrics.

> *Take me by the tongue and I'll know you*
> *You wanted control so we waited*
> *I put on a show now we're naked*

Tongue kissing and getting naked? Really! The artist goes on to mention that his girl didn't want sex so he pretended like it was cool with him only to talk her into doing it later. You can miss a lot when you don't examine the lyrics.

When I looked at all 20 songs and read the lyrics, I realized that 16 out of the 20 had references to sex, alcohol or drugs or violence; and the references were **not** subtle.

So, that was 2011. Let's look at Billboard's top 20 songs of 2015. They are:

1. See You Again – Wiz Khalifa
2. Cheerleader – OMI
3. Watch Me – Silento
4. Bad Blood – Taylor Swift featuring Kendrick Lamar
5. Trap Queen – Fetty Wap
6. Can't Feel My Face – The Weekend
7. Shut Up and Dance – Walk the Moon
8. Where Are U Now – Skrillex & Diplo with Justin Bieber
9. Hey Mama – David Guetta featuring Nicki Minaij, Bebe Rexha and Afrojack
10. Fight Song - Rachel Platten
11. Honey, I'm Good – Andy Grammer
12. Uptown Funk – Mark Ronson featuring Bruno Mars
13. Want to Want Me – Jason Derulo
14. Worth It – Fifth Harmony featuring Kid Ink
15. B**** Better Have My Money – Rihanna
16. Earned It – The Weekend
17. Good For You – Selena Gomez featuring A$AP Rocky
18. Lean On – Major Lazer & DJ Snake featuring M0
19. The Hills – The Weekend
20. Post to Be – Omarion featuring Chris Brown and Jhene Aika

See any songs you like on the list? How do you

think those songs compare to the list of 2011? Let's find out.

Of the 20 songs on the list, eight reference sex, seven contain profanity, and one references drugs. So, in comparison, the list of 2015 contains fewer negative references, but more than half contain either sex, alcohol or drugs. A little disappointing. On a positive note, one of the songs, *Honey, I'm Good* by Andy Grammer promotes being faithful. Here are some of the lyrics:

So nah nah honey, I'm good
I could have another but I probably should not
I got somebody at home,
And if I stay I might not leave alone
No, honey, I'm good
I could have another but I probably should not
I gotta bid you adieu
To another I will stay true

This study and others like it show that there is a link between the music you listen to and the thoughts and beliefs you have. It's almost impossible to listen to lyrics about sex and not think about sex. It's virtually impossible to sing a song about getting your drink on and backin' that thang up without visualizing it. The more you expose yourself to these types of lyrics, the more desensitized you become to the damaging behavior promoted in them. Repeated exposure makes your brain think, *"Eh, no big deal!"*

I have a challenge for you. I want you to choose three songs that you have on your phone or mp3. Google the lyrics and see how many lines reference sex, alcohol or drugs. Pay attention to the images that pop into your mind as you're reading the lyrics. Then, ask yourself, "Do I really want to keep this song on my playlist?"

Lie #4: It's Just a Song
Truth: The Lyrics Seep In

12
Lie #5: Everybody's Doing It

What percentage of teens in the U.S. do you think are having sex? 70%? 80? Try less than 50%! Research shows that about 47% of high school students in the U.S. have had sex. Does that number surprise you? I definitely thought it was higher. The fact is, fewer teens are engaging in sexual activity now than twenty years ago. In the 1980s, about 51% of girls and 60% of boys were sexually active. Compare that to the 44% or girls and 47% of boys that are sexually active today. Even though sex is more "in your face" today than it was in the 80s, more teens today are armed with the facts about sex and are making better choices.

Ladies, I can't just tell you to keep your legs closed. I have to tell you *why* not having sex *is* the best decision to make. You know it's against God's will and you know it's not Christian-like, but is that enough to keep you from actually doing it? You need all the facts.

You need to know *why* most girls have sex in the first place so you can avoid those situations. You also need to know that you are influenced by the images you see and things you hear in the media that sensationalize sex. The reason I thought more teens were having sex was because of what I've seen and heard in the media. No one is immune.

The media bombards you with images that sensationalize sexuality. You are lead to believe that everybody's having sex. Forty-eight percent is far from everyone. This lie creates an unspoken peer pressure that communicates the message that it's okay for you to have sex.

Pre-marital sex is explained away by many rationales. Here are some of them.

Rationale #1: I Can Protect Myself From Pregnancy.

There are more methods of birth control out now than ever before. Pills, foams, patches, condoms, implants – they're all available and can protect you from getting pregnant. But, know the truth. They all come with risks and **none** are 100% guaranteed to keep you baby free.

The Pill - 92-97% effective – no protection against STDs (sexually transmitted diseases) – side effects: nausea, headaches, blood clots – must be taken at the same time everyday

Condoms – 84% effective – helps prevent STDs – possibility of latex allergic reaction – can break or be defective and allow sperm to pass through

Withdrawal (pulling out) – 78% effective – little control (totally up to the guy) – no protection against STDs – pre-ejaculation can contain sperm and cause pregnancy

The Patch – 92% - no protection for STDs – must be replaced weekly – possible skin irritation – visible

Emergency Contraception (Morning After Pill) – 89% effective – no protection for STDs – must be taken right after sex – can cause nausea, vomiting and irregular bleeding – expensive

Foam, Jelly, Suppository – 74% effective – can leak – messiness may discourage use

Abstinence – 100% effective – prevents STDs - no side effects – no cost – can be difficult, but not impossible!

As you can see, all these methods come with their challenges, including abstinence. But, abstinence is the only option that has zero side effects. Great for the body (no babies), the soul (no soul ties) and the spirit (what God wants). At the end of the day, you and only you are making this decision, so be informed.

Rationale #2: I Love Him and He Loves Me

Ever heard the song *What's Love Got to Do with It?* Well actually, it has a lot to do with it! As women, we are more emotional than guys. We often make decisions based on how we feel. That can sometimes be a good thing, but it can also get us into trouble with the opposite sex.

It's a lot easier to say no to sex when you're just not feeling a guy. But if you really think he's the one and you're head over heels in love, it's hard to say no. Sometimes, he might think sex will solidify the relationship or take it to the next level. You might think that kind of intimacy will make the relationship stronger and more mature as well. Have you ever thought, *"If I sleep with him, he'll be satisfied and won't want anybody else."* You could be right. You also could be very wrong. The thing is, you won't know until you do it, and if you're wrong, it's too late. Sex can't be undone.

Sometimes guys will say they want sex, but after it happens, they don't want you. The idea of being intimate with someone is exciting, but once it happens, the novelty can wear off. Sex can become commonplace and lose the excitement it had at first. Guys can feel bored; like they've conquered the challenge. And now it's time to find a new one.

Things don't always turn out that way, but they can and often do. Is it worth the risk? Is it worth the heartache and confusion that you'll be left to deal with? Most girls that have had sex say it was not worth the consequences it brought them. Remember the letters from the teenage girls? They're real.

Rationale #3: I Just Want to See What It's Like

You've seen it on TV and you've heard about it in love songs. But what's sex really like? Being curious about sex is totally normal. There isn't a girl on the planet that hasn't wondered what it's *really* like. We've already talked about how sex is sensationalized into this whirlwind, mind blowing experience, but is all that talk for real?

If you hear your friends talking about the amazing sexual experiences they've had, don't be impressed. Teens often exaggerate about their sexual experiences because they think it sounds impressive. Chances are they're embellishing what actually happened or making the whole thing up altogether! So, don't have sex for the sake of seeing what's it's like. Everybody's experience if different, but for girls, the first time is uncomfortable at best.

God intended sex to be between husband and wife. It's a pleasurable experience when you're married partly because you have infinite, guilt-free opportunities to engage in it. You're not doing it to see what it's like, to hold onto your man or to fit in with the crowd.

Some of you have already lost your virginity. Even though you're not a virgin, you're still a daughter of the

King! O, don't think, *"Well, I'm not a virgin anymore, so what does it matter if I keep on having sex? Guys are going to expect me to have sex with them."* Learn from your past experiences by making a different choice next time. You may not be a virgin, but you can still be pure in the eyes of God by choosing abstinence now. Ask God for forgiveness and keep moving forward.

God loves you and wants you to wait until you're married to have sex. So, do everything you can to wait. Know exactly what you will say and do if you find yourself in a tempting situation. Know the risks you take if you choose to have sex: pregnancy, STDs, soul ties, shame . . . the list goes on and on. Know the tremendous feeling of pride you'll wake up with in the morning, after you've made the decision to say no the night before. Most of all, know how to see yourself through the lens of Christ.

The best thing about not having sex is knowing 100% without a doubt that you are *not* pregnant, *don't* have an STD, and *won't* feel like a fool because you gave it up yesterday and he's with somebody else today! Remember, everybody's **NOT** doing it!

Lie #5: Everybody's Doing It
Truth: Everybody's NOT Doing It

Final Thoughts

Ladies, I have thoroughly enjoyed writing this book for you! I hope that you will use the knowledge and tools I've shared with you to live your best life, as a virtuous young lady for Christ!

Before you close the pages of this book, I encourage you to say a prayer and ask God to help you use what you've learned to live a virtuous life. Pray that He will help you use these practices in your everyday life starting right now. Keep this book in a place where you can easily find it. Go back to it when in you're in those sticky situations and remind yourself of what God says. Look back on these pages when you have to make a tough decision and aren't sure what to do. Use the Bible verses in this book to dig deeper into God's word and find out what blessings He has in store for you. As you walk with God and develop your relationship with Him know that you are virtuous, victorious and valued!

Contact Me

I'd love to hear from you! Visit my website at **write4queenz.com**. You can also find me on Facebook at **www.facebook.com/write4queenz**.

Email your pic with one of my books and I'll feature you on my Reader's Wall of Fame! Send your pic to **write4queenz@gmail.com**. Get a FREE subscription to my online magazine, *Virtuous Victorious & Valued.* Just click on the subscribe link on my website.

About the Author

Angela Whitehead is a Christian author whose mission is to help young ladies see themselves through the lens of Christ. Angela writes books that inspire and encourage young women to be virtuous, victorious and valued! She has written two fiction books entitled *Whose Am I*? and *Selfish Faith*, and Virtuous Victorious & Valued, a guidebook for teenage girls.

Angela is the founder of Write 4 Queenz, a publishing company that produces literature that inspires young ladies to see themselves through the lens of Christ. She conducts workshops for teenage girls and publishes a free online magazine called Virtuous Victorious & Valued. Angela is an Assistant Principal at a middle school in the Atlanta Metro-Area. She resides in Acworth, GA with her husband Norris and two children, Niya and Isaiah.

Sources

1. "2014 Plastic Surgery Statistics Report Quick Facts." Plastic Surgery.org. American Society of Plastic Surgeons, 15 May 2014. Web. 17 July 2015. **<http://www.plasticsurgery.org/news/plastic-surgery-statistics/2014-statistics.html>.**

2. A Christian Guys Plea [Motion picture]. (2014). US.

3. A Plan for Abstinence- Sex Can Wait [Motion picture]. (2008). US: Sex Can Wait.org.

4. Ackerman, T. (2012, April 5). 6. Popular Song Lyrics Contain Sex, Alcohol and No Regrets. Retrieved July 9, 2015, from **http://www.deseretnews.com/article/865553547/Popular-song-lyrics-contain-sex-alcohol-and-no-regrets.html?pg=all**

5. Alfonsi, S., & Fahy, U. (2009, April 7). Steve Harvey: Don't Be Stupid About Men. Retrieved July 17, 2015, from **http://abcnews.go.com/Entertainment/story?id=7272481.**

6. Andersen, K. (2015, April 16). Data Shows Homosexuality Hugely Overrepresented on the Big Screen, but GLADD says it's Still Not Enough. Retrieved July 14, 2015, from **https://www.lifesitenews.com/news/data-shows-homosexuals-hugely-overrepresented-on-the-big-screen-but-glaad-s**
7. Birth Control Comparison Chart. (2013, January 12). Retrieved July 19, 2015, from **http://www.ashasexualhealth.org/pdfs/ContraceptiveOptions.pdf**

8. Cohn, D., Passel, J., & Wang, W. (2011, December 14). Barely Half of US Adults Are Married – A Record Low. Retrieved July 17, 2015, from **http://www.pewsocialtrends.org/2011/12/14/barely-half-of-u-s-adults-are-married-a-record-low/**

9. Crooks, R. (2013, April 11). Splurge Vs. Save: Which Beauty Products are Worth the Extra Cost? Retrieved July 15, 2015, from **https://blog.mint.com/consumer-iq/splurge-vs-save-which-beauty-products-are-worth-the-extra-cost-0413/**

10. Generation M2: Media in the Lives of 8- to 18-Year-Olds." *Kaiser Family Foundation.org*. Kaiser Family Foundation, 20 Jan. 2010. Web. 14 July 2015.

11. Godfrey, B. (2015, February 14). Myths and the Truth. Retrieved July 15, 2015, from 1. **http:www.pamf.org/teen/sex/pregnancy/myths.html#Myths & the Truth**

12. History and Timeline of the Freedom to Marry in the United States. (2015, July 1). Retrieved July 13, 2015, from **http://www.freedomtomarry.org/pages/history-and-timeline-of-marriage**

13. Is This Relationship Unhealthy? w/ Dharius Daniels [Motion picture]. (2014). US: Redefined TV.
14. Jill Scott and Son Cover Ebony Magazine. (2013, April 1). Retrieved July 17, 2015, from **http://www.blackcelebkids.com/2013/04/01/jill-scott-and-son-cover-ebony-magazine/**

15. KBCs Modesty Project [Motion picture]. (2013). US: Evangel Ize.

16. Killing Us Softly 4: Trailer [Motion picture]. (2012). Mediaed.org.

17. Lopez, M., & Gonzales-Barrera, A. (2014, March 6). 11. Women's College Enrollment Gains Leave Men Behind. Retrieved July 17, 2015, from **http://www.pewresearch.org/fact-tank/2014/03/06/womens-college-enrollment-gains-leave-men-behind/**

18. Martinez, Gladys, and Joyce Abma. "Sexual Activity, Contraceptive Use, and Childbearing of Teenagers Ages 15-19 in the United States." Centers for Disease Control and Prevention. National Center for Health Statistics, 20 Nov. 2015. Web. 16 July 2015. **<http://www.cdc.gov/nchs/data/databriefs/db209.htm>.**

19. Models Without Makeup [Motion picture]. (2014). Ocio TV.

20. Modesty: Redefined TV [Motion picture]. (2014). US: Redefined TV.
21. Nia Long Graces the Essence April Cover. (2014, April 13). Retrieved July 17, 2015, from **http://www.essence.com/2014/03/06/nia-long-essence-cover**

22. Paquette, D., & Cai, W. (2015, July 22). Why American Teenagers are Having Much Less Sex. Retrieved August 6, 2015, from **http://www.washingtonpost.com/news/wonkblog/wp/2015/07/22/why-american-teenagers-are-having-much-less-sex/**

23. The Secret to Looking Absolutely Perfect [Motion picture]. (2014).

24. Snow, J. (2015, January 21). Agent of Change: A Q&A with GLAAD's Sarah Kate Ellis. Retrieved July 11, 2015, from **http://www.metroweekly.com/2015/01/agent-of-change-sarah-kate-ellis-of-glaad/**

25. The 2014 State of Women-Owned Businesses Report. (2014, August 16). Retrieved July 17, 2015.

26. "The Highest-Rated Series of 2014 – and How People Watched Them." The Hollywood Reporter.com. The Hollywood Reporter, 30 Dec. 2014. Web. 17 July 2014. **<http://www.hollywoodreporter.com/live-feed/highest-rated-broadcast-series-2014-760484>.**

27. "The Hot 100." Billboard.com. Billboard, 4 July 2015. Web. 17 July 2015. **<http://www.billboard.com/charts/hot-100>.**

28. Try Colbie Caillat [Motion picture]. (2014). US.

NOTES:

NOTES:

NOTES:

NOTES:

NOTES:

NOTES:

NOTES:

NOTES:

NOTES:

NOTES:

NOTES:

NOTES:

www.ingramcontent.com/pod-product-compliance
Lightning Source LLC
Chambersburg PA
CBHW062005040426
42447CB00010B/1918
* 9 7 8 0 6 9 2 3 9 6 7 0 4 *